HEALTHY CHOICES

Breakfast

Vic Parker

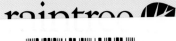

Raintree is an imprint of Capstone Global Library Limited, a company incorporated in England and Wales having its registered office at 7 Pilgrim Street, London EC4V 6LB – Registered company number: 6695582

www.raintreepublishers.co.uk
myorders@raintreepublishers.co.uk

Edited by Rebecca Rissman, Dan Nunn, and
    Diyan Leake
Designed by Philippa Jenkins
Original illustrations © Capstone Global
    Library Ltd 2014
Picture research by Tracy Cummins
Production by Helen McCreath
Originated by Capstone Global Library Ltd
Printed and bound in China

ISBN 978 1 406 27195 9 (hardback)
17 16 15 14 13
10 9 8 7 6 5 4 3 2 1

ISBN 978 1 406 27200 0 (paperback)
18 17 16 15 14
10 9 8 7 6 5 4 3 2 1

Parker, Vic
Breakfast (Healthy Choices)
A full catalogue record for this book is available from the British Library.

Acknowledgements
We would like to thank the following for permission to reproduce photographs: Capstone Publishers (Karon Dubke) pp. 6, 7, 8, 9, 10, 11, 12, 13, 14, 15, 16, 17, 18, 19, 20, 21, 22, 23, 24, 25, 26, 27; Getty Images p. 4 (Shannon Fagan), Shutterstock p. 5 (© bikeriderlondon).

Cover photograph of a bowl of children's cereal and milk reproduced with permission of Shutterstock (© Hong Vo) and wholewheat cereal with fruit reproduced with permission of Getty Images (Donald Erickson).

Every effort has been made to contact copyright holders of material reproduced in this book. Any omissions will be rectified in subsequent printings if notice is given to the publisher.

All the internet addresses (URLs) given in this book were valid at the time of going to press. However, due to the dynamic nature of the internet, some addresses may have changed, or sites may have changed or ceased to exist since publication. While the author and publisher regret any inconvenience this may cause readers, no responsibility for any such changes can be accepted by either the author or the publisher.

Contents

Some words are shown in bold, **like this.** You can find out what they mean by looking in the glossary.

Why make healthy choices?

Your body runs on food and water. You need food to think, move, and grow. Healthy foods give your body lots of goodness. However, if you eat unhealthy foods, you will not feel or look your best.

Eating healthy foods can help your body fight disease.

Don't forget to brush
after meals to keep
your teeth healthy!

toothbrush

Your body needs different kinds of
foods, in the right amounts for your
age and size, to work properly. If you
eat healthy foods, you will have lots of
energy. You will be able to think quickly
and clearly. You will look good, too.

What makes a breakfast healthy or unhealthy?

It is important to eat breakfast to wake your body up after sleeping and get it going again. Some breakfasts are much less healthy than others. For instance, bagels can be high in **sodium**, which is bad for your heart.

Buttery croissants are high in **saturated fat**, which can damage your heart and blood vessels.

2 slices of **wholemeal** toast with unsweetened fruit spread
300 calories

2 slices of wholemeal toast with chocolate hazelnut spread
550 calories

The energy food gives is measured in **calories**. Everyone needs a certain amount of calories per day to stay healthy, depending on your age, your size, and how active you are. However, eating too many calories at meals and snack times can make you **overweight**.

Processed cereals

Cereals are a great breakfast choice, since they give us lots of energy. However, many cereals made especially for children are high in sugar and **calories**. Some healthy-looking breakfast cereals are also high in **sodium**.

Full-fat milk makes your breakfast high in unhealthy **saturated fat**.

full-fat milk

added sodium

high in fat

added artificial **colourings**

added sugar

Semi-skimmed milk and skimmed milk are healthy choices.

skimmed milk

bran cereal

wheat cereal

Wholegrain cereals contain slow-release energy, which keeps us going for longer. They are packed with the **vitamins** and **minerals** your body needs to grow and repair itself. They are a good source of **fibre**, which keeps your **digestive system** in good order.

Muesli, granola, and porridge

Muesli and granola both contain healthy whole grains, nuts, fruits, and seeds. However, shop-bought granola is toasted in oil and sugar, which makes it high in fat and **calories**. Muesli is raw, but many shop-bought mueslis contain a lot of added sugar and **sodium**.

muesli with added sugar and sodium

Some muesli and granola can contain more sugar than sugar-frosted breakfast cereal.

granola baked in sugar and hydrogenated vegetable oil

muesli with raw nuts and dried fruit

granola baked in maple syrup and olive oil

porridge, honey, nuts, raisins

Make your porridge with semi-skimmed or skimmed milk to keep the fat content down.

It is easy to make healthier muesli and granola at home. Always use raw nuts and seeds, and rely on just dried fruit for sweetness instead of sugar. Porridge is a very healthy choice of hot **wholegrain** cereal.

Toast

Bread is a good food choice for breakfast since it contains **carbohydrates** that give us energy. However, some types of bread are much healthier than others. **Wholemeal** bread has **fibre, vitamins,** and **minerals** in it. In white bread, much of this goodness has been taken out.

jam

butter

white toast

White bread with butter and jam is fatty and sugary without much goodness for your body.

Wholemeal bread is also healthier because it gives us energy that is released slowly. Use low-fat spread on toast instead of high-fat butter. Unsweetened fruit purée is better for you than sugary jam.

For an even healthier choice, do without any fatty spread and just have the fruity topping.

mashed banana

fruit topping

wholemeal bread

Eggs

Some foods, such as meat, fish, chicken, and beans, are rich sources of **protein**. Your body needs protein to make skin, muscle, and other tissues. Eggs are high in protein but they can also be high in fat if they are cooked in an unhealthy way.

Eggs can be good for us, but not if unhealthy ingredients are added.

high-fat butter

added high-fat cheese

white toast

scrambled eggs fried in high-fat butter

Eggs are rich in **antioxidants**. These are natural substances which strengthen the body's ability to fight disease.

hard-boiled egg

low-fat spread

wholemeal toast

Eggs cooked in a low-fat way are an excellent breakfast choice. Like other protein foods, eggs take longer to go through the **digestive system** and can keep you feeling fuller for longer. Eggs are also rich in **vitamins** and **minerals**.

Breakfast sandwiches

Fast-food breakfast sandwiches can look tempting but they are usually high in **saturated fat**, **sodium**, and **calories**. Also, nearly everything in them is **processed** and they may have unhealthy **artificial additives**.

Processed foods may have **flavouring**, **colouring**, and **preservatives** added to them. These are **chemicals** that have little goodness and can even be harmful.

processed white flour

fatty fried egg

processed cheese

processed sausage meat

You can help to make a healthier breakfast sandwich at home. Use **wholemeal** bread for slow-release energy, **fibre**, **vitamins**, and **minerals**. Top it with low-fat ingredients, such as grilled tomatoes or mushrooms, and a **poached** egg or **lean** meat for **protein**.

A homemade breakfast sandwich can be both healthy and delicious.

wholemeal muffin

lean bacon

poached egg

Pancakes and waffles

Pancakes and waffles are both made from batter containing milk, eggs, and flour. If full-fat milk and white flour are used, the pancakes and waffles become high in fat (especially if fried in oil) and low in **vitamins** and **minerals.**

white flour, sugary
syrup, high-fat
whipped cream

white flour,
sugary syrup,
sugary jam

Unhealthy toppings
are often added to
pancakes and waffles.

blueberries

strawberries

maple syrup

oatmeal pancakes

low-fat natural yoghurt

wholemeal-flour waffles

Use just a little maple syrup to add sweetness without too many **calories**.

Pancakes and waffles are healthier if they are made with **wholemeal** flour and lower-fat milk. Add extra goodness with healthy toppings such as fresh fruit, low-fat natural yoghurt, and maple syrup, a natural sweetener containing many **nutrients** that fight disease.

19

Fruity breakfasts

Fruit is full of **vitamins** and **minerals**. However, it is not healthy when it is turned into high-sugar jam in layers of high-fat pastry, like a pop tart.

sugary jam, artificial **colouring**

pastry high in **saturated fat**

Pop tarts are a high-calorie breakfast choice, with little goodness for your body.

Rice cakes are filling and keep you from feeling hungry.

unsweetened raspberry purée

mashed banana

rice cake

peanut butter

strawberries, blueberries, and low-fat yoghurt

Rice cakes will give you the crunch of a pop tart but they are much lower in fat and **calories.** Choose the unflavoured type and add your own fruity toppings for lots of vitamins, minerals, and **fibre** – either unsweetened fruit purées or chopped fresh fruit.

Cooked breakfasts

On a cold day, a big cooked breakfast can warm you and fill you up till lunchtime. It can give you energy, **protein, vitamins, minerals,** and **antioxidants.** However, if your cooked breakfast is fried, it can be a meal incredibly high in **saturated fat** and **calories.**

Using an animal fat such as butter for frying is an unhealthy cooking method.

fried hash browns

fried fatty bacon

fried eggs

fried pork sausage

wholemeal toast with low-fat spread

grilled lean bacon

A cooked breakfast can be healthy.

poached eggs

grilled vegetarian sausage

For a healthier breakfast, cook **lean** meat using low-fat cooking methods such as grilling and poaching. Swap your meat sausage for a vegetarian sausage, to add vitamins, minerals, and **fibre**. Swap hash browns for **wholemeal** toast to give you energy that is slowly released through the morning.

Drinks

Milk contains **calcium** for strong bones and teeth, and **protein** for healthy skin and muscles. Fruit juices are packed with **vitamins** and **minerals**. However, some milk is high in fat, and shop-bought fruit juices can have lots of added sugar.

Full-fat milk and shop-bought juices can be quite high in **calories**.

fruit **concentrate**, with added syrup, sugar

whole milk

Swap full-fat milk for semi-skimmed or skimmed to get all the health benefits, with less fat and sugar. Even fresh fruit juice is not as good as eating the whole fruit, so just have it in small amounts. Water is always a great choice of drink. Every bit of your body needs water to work properly.

lower-fat semi-skimmed milk

low-fat skimmed milk

Unsweetened drinks are much better for your teeth than sugary drinks.

water

fresh fruit juice

Food quiz

Take a look at these breakfasts. Can you work out which picture shows an unhealthy breakfast and which shows a healthy breakfast, and why?

spinach and mushroom omelette fried in a little sunflower oil

water

wholemeal toast with low-fat spread

breakfast pizza topped with cheesy scrambled eggs and fried bacon and sausage bits

shop-bought fruit smoothie

The answer is on the next page.

Food quiz answers

This is the healthy breakfast. The vegetable omelette is high in **protein**, **vitamins**, **minerals**, and **antioxidants**. The **wholemeal** toast will give you **fibre**, vitamins, minerals, and energy that is slowly released. Water is essential for everything in your body to work properly.

This is the unhealthy breakfast. White-flour pizza dough is high in **sodium** and lacks fibre, vitamins, and minerals. Cheesy scrambled eggs and fried bacon and sausage bits are high in **saturated fat**. Shop-bought smoothies can be packed with sugar, fat, and **artificial additives**. Did you guess correctly?

Tips for healthy eating

Use this eatwell plate guide to choose the right amounts of different foods for good health. Choose low-fat cooking methods and do not add salt (it is high in **sodium**). Don't forget to drink several glasses of water and to exercise every day.

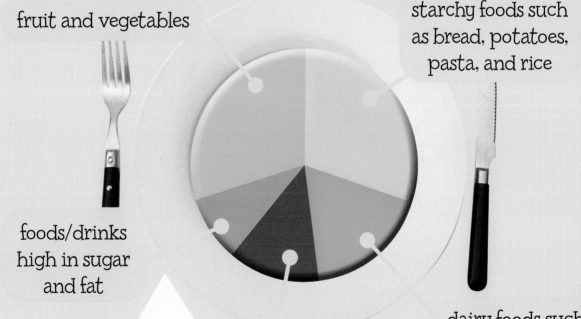

fruit and vegetables

starchy foods such as bread, potatoes, pasta, and rice

foods/drinks high in sugar and fat

dairy foods such as milk, yoghurt, and cheese

See if you can get the right balance over the course of a whole day.

protein foods such as meat, fish, eggs and beans

Glossary

antioxidant substance that helps your body fight off disease

artificial additive man-made substance that is added to food, such as colouring, flavouring, and preservatives

calcium a mineral that your body needs to build strong bones and teeth. Calcium is found in dairy foods and some vegetables, nuts, and seeds.

calorie unit we use for measuring energy

carbohydrate substance in starchy foods (such as potatoes, pasta, and rice) and sugary foods that gives you energy

chemical substance made by mixing other substances together

colouring something added to food to make it look attractive

concentrate juice that has had most of the water taken out so that it lasts longer

digestive system all the body parts that break down food so the body can use it

fibre part of certain plants that passes through your body without being broken down. Fibre helps other foods to pass through your stomach, too. Some fibre can also help your blood stay healthy.

flavouring something added to food to make it taste nicer

lean describes meat that has little fat or has had the fatty bits trimmed off

mineral natural substance, such as iron, that is essential for health

nutrient substance in food that is good for your body, such as vitamins, minerals, and antioxidants

overweight heavier than is healthy for your age and height

poach cook using the method of simmering a whole piece of food (such as an egg or a fillet of fish) in water

preservative something added to food to make it last longer

processed made or prepared in a factory. Processed foods may contain artificial additives.

protein natural substance that your body needs to build skin, muscle, and other tissues. Protein is found in foods such as meat, fish, and beans.

saturated fat type of fat found in butter, fatty cuts of meat, cheese, and cream. It is bad for your heart and blood vessels.

sodium a natural substance found in salt

vitamin natural substance that is essential for good health

wholegrain, wholemeal made using every part of the grain, without removing any of the inner or outer bits

31

Find out more

Books

All About Cereals (Food Zone), Vic Parker (QED, 2010)
All About Dairy (Food Zone), Vic Parker (QED, 2010)
Build Your Own Breakfast Sticker Activity Book, Susan
Shaw-Russell (Dover Publications, 2011)

Websites

Try some healthy recipes at: **www.bbcgoodfood.com/content/
recipes/healthy/healthy-kids**

Try some healthy eating activities at: **www.familylearning.org.
uk/balanced_diet.html** and **www.bbc.co.uk/northernireland/
schools/4_11/uptoyou/index.shtml**

Find out more about the eatwell plate healthy eating guidelines
at: **www.nhs.uk/Livewell/Goodfood/Pages/eatwell-plate.aspx**

Index